Building the Perfect Relationship: A Comprehensive Guide

Jackquelin Grant

Published by Jackquelin Grant, 2024.

While every precaution has been taken in the preparation of this book, the publisher assumes no responsibility for errors or omissions, or for damages resulting from the use of the information contained herein.

BUILDING THE PERFECT RELATIONSHIP: A COMPREHENSIVE GUIDE

First edition. February 22, 2024.

Copyright © 2024 Jackquelin Grant.

ISBN: 979-8224829439

Written by Jackquelin Grant.

Table of Contents

Building the Perfect
RELATIONSHIP
A Comprehensive Guide

Jackquelin M. Grant, MA, MHC-LP, DBH

Jackquelin M. Grant, MA, MHC-LP, DBH

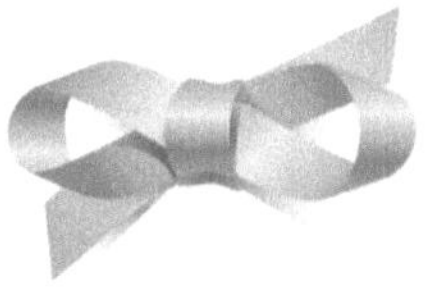

Chapter 1:

Introduction to Building the Perfect Relationship

The Importance of Relationships

Relationships form the fabric of human existence, shaping our experiences, emotions, and overall well-being. In this chapter, we delve into the significance of relationships, exploring why they matter deeply in our lives.

Understanding Human Connection

At our core, humans are social beings. From birth, we seek connection with others, starting with our caregivers and expanding to include friends, family, romantic partners, and communities. These connections fulfill our innate need for belonging, companionship, and support.

Emotional Fulfillment and Support

Relationships provide us with emotional nourishment and support during both triumphs and tribulations. They offer a safe space to express our true selves, share our joys and sorrows, and feel understood and validated. Through meaningful connections, we experience a sense of belonging and acceptance, which contributes to our overall happiness and well-being.

Enhanced Resilience and Coping Mechanisms

Strong relationships act as a buffer against life's challenges, providing us with the strength and resilience to navigate difficult times. When we face adversity, having a support system in place can mitigate stress, alleviate loneliness, and offer practical assistance and guidance. Moreover, knowing that we have someone to lean on during tough times instills a sense of security and confidence in our ability to overcome obstacles.

Promoting Physical Health

BUILDING THE PERFECT RELATIONSHIP: A COMPREHENSIVE GUIDE

Believe it or not, healthy relationships can benefit our physical health. Research has shown that individuals in supportive and loving relationships tend to have lower rates of chronic illness, reduced levels of stress hormones, and improved immune function. Relationships' emotional comfort and stability contribute to lower blood pressure, better cardiovascular health, and overall longevity.

Fostering Personal Growth and Development

In addition to providing emotional and physical support, relationships catalyze personal growth and development. Through interactions with others, we gain valuable insights into ourselves, learn essential life skills such as communication and compromise, and are encouraged to step out of our comfort zones. Whether through the challenges of resolving conflicts or the joys of shared accomplishments, relationships offer endless opportunities for learning and self-discovery.

Conclusion

In essence, relationships are the cornerstone of a fulfilling and meaningful life. They provide love, support, and companionship, enriching our experiences and shaping our identities. By recognizing the importance of relationships and nurturing them with care and intentionality, we can cultivate deeper connections and lead more fulfilling lives.

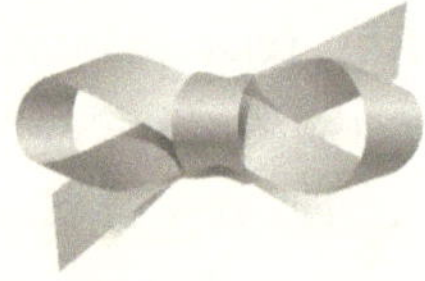

Understanding the Dynamics of Healthy Relationships

Healthy relationships are not simply a matter of chance; they are cultivated through understanding, effort, and commitment. In this chapter, we explore the intricate dynamics underpinning healthy relationships, shedding light on the key components contributing to their success.

Clear and Open Communication

Effective communication is the cornerstone of any healthy relationship. It involves expressing one's thoughts and feelings and actively listening and empathizing with one's partner. Clear and open communication fosters understanding, builds trust, and strengthens emotional intimacy. It allows partners to address issues constructively, resolve conflicts, and nurture a sense of connection and mutual respect.

Mutual Trust and Respect

Trust and respect are fundamental pillars of a healthy relationship. Trust entails believing in your partner's integrity, reliability, and loyalty, while respect involves valuing their thoughts, feelings, and boundaries. In a healthy relationship, partners trust each other implicitly, feel safe being vulnerable, and uphold each other's dignity and autonomy. Trust and respect create a solid foundation upon which emotional intimacy and mutual support can thrive.

Empathy and Compassion

Empathy—the ability to understand and share another person's feelings—and compassion—the desire to alleviate their suffering—are essential qualities in healthy relationships. When partners demonstrate empathy and compassion towards each other, they foster a deep sense of connection and emotional intimacy. They offer support and validation during distress, celebrate each other's successes, and demonstrate a genuine interest in each other's well-being.

Shared Values and Goals

Alignment in values, goals, and priorities is crucial for the long-term success of a relationship. Partners with shared values and aspirations are better equipped to navigate life's challenges and pursue their dreams together. They collaborate as a team, make decisions collectively, and support each other's personal growth and development. Shared values create a sense of unity and purpose, strengthening the bond between partners and fostering a more profound understanding of connection.

Boundaries and Autonomy

Respecting each other's boundaries and autonomy is essential for maintaining a healthy balance in a relationship. Partners should feel empowered to express their needs, set boundaries, and pursue their interests and goals. Healthy relationships allow for independence and self-expression while nurturing interdependence and mutual support. Respecting boundaries demonstrates trust, promotes self-esteem, and fosters a sense of agency and empowerment within the relationship.

Conclusion

Understanding the dynamics of healthy relationships requires a commitment to fostering clear communication, mutual trust and respect, empathy and compassion, shared values and goals, and boundaries and autonomy. By cultivating these key components, partners can build strong, resilient relationships characterized by love, support, and mutual fulfillment.

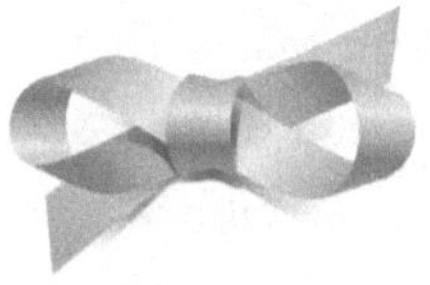

Chapter 2:

Foundations of a Perfect Relationship

Communication: The Key to Connection

Communication serves as the lifeblood of any relationship, providing the means through which partners express their thoughts, feelings, and needs and connect on a deeper level. This chapter delves into the importance of effective communication in fostering connections and strengthening relationships.

The Power of Effective Communication

Effective communication is more than just exchanging words; it involves active listening, empathy, and clarity of expression. It forms the foundation upon which emotional intimacy and understanding are built. Through effective communication, partners can share their joys and sorrows, resolve conflicts, and express love and appreciation, strengthening their bond.

Active Listening

Active listening is a cornerstone of effective communication. It entails giving full attention to your partner, being present in the moment, and seeking to understand their perspective without judgment or interruption. By listening attentively, validating their feelings, and reflecting on what you've heard, you demonstrate respect and empathy, fostering a more profound sense of connection and mutual understanding.

Expressing Needs and Emotions

Openly expressing needs and emotions is essential for fostering intimacy and trust. When partners feel safe being vulnerable and sharing their innermost thoughts and feelings, they deepen their emotional connection and strengthen their bond. Encouraging open and honest communication creates a supportive environment where partners can validate each other's experiences and work together to address their needs and concerns.

Effective Conflict Resolution

Conflict is inevitable in any relationship, but how it is managed can make all the difference. Effective conflict resolution involves approaching disagreements with empathy, respect, and a willingness to find mutually beneficial solutions. It requires active listening, assertive communication, and a focus on problem-solving rather than blame or criticism. By constructively navigating conflicts, partners can strengthen their relationships and emerge more robust and resilient.

Nonverbal Communication

Nonverbal communication, including body language, tone of voice, and facial expressions, plays a significant role in conveying emotions and intentions. Partners should recognize nonverbal cues and align their verbal and nonverbal messages to ensure clear and consistent communication. Being attuned to each other's nonverbal signals enhances understanding and strengthens the connection between partners.

Continuous Improvement

Communication skills are not innate; they require practice, patience, and ongoing effort to develop and refine. Partners should commit to continuously improving their communication skills through active listening, empathetic expression, and constructive feedback. By prioritizing open and honest communication, partners can nurture a robust, resilient relationship built on trust, understanding, and mutual respect.

Conclusion

Communication is the cornerstone of a healthy and fulfilling relationship, serving as the key to connection and intimacy. By cultivating practical communication skills, partners can deepen their bond, navigate challenges, and foster a relationship characterized by trust, empathy, and mutual support.

Trust: Building the Bedrock

Trust is the cornerstone of any healthy relationship, serving as the foundation upon which intimacy, security, and mutual respect are built. In this chapter, we explore the significance of trust in fostering strong and resilient relationships and strategies for building and maintaining trust between partners.

Understanding Trust

Trust is the belief in another person's reliability, integrity, and goodwill. It involves having confidence that your partner will act in your best interests, honor their commitments, and remain faithful and loyal. Trust creates a sense of security and emotional safety within the relationship, allowing partners to be vulnerable, express themselves freely, and deepen their emotional connection.

Transparency and Honesty

Transparency and honesty are essential for building trust in a relationship. Partners should be open and forthcoming about their thoughts, feelings, and actions, even when difficult or uncomfortable. Being honest with each other fosters authenticity and integrity, demonstrating a commitment to building a relationship based on trust and mutual respect.

Consistency and Reliability

Consistency and reliability are critical components of trustworthiness. Partners should demonstrate reliability by following through on their promises and commitments, being there for each other in need, and consistently upholding shared values and expectations. Consistency builds a sense of predictability and stability within the relationship, reinforcing trust and deepening the emotional bond between partners.

Vulnerability and Empathy

Vulnerability and empathy are crucial in building trust and intimacy in a relationship. Partners should feel safe being vulnerable, sharing their fears, insecurities, and weaknesses without fear of judgment or rejection. By demonstrating empathy and compassion towards each other's struggles and insecurities, partners create a supportive environment where trust can flourish.

Forgiveness and Repair

Conflict and mistakes are inevitable in any relationship, but how they are addressed can strengthen or undermine trust. Partners should be willing to forgive each other's transgressions, apologize when necessary, and actively work towards repairing any breaches of trust. By acknowledging mistakes, taking responsibility for their actions, and making amends, partners demonstrate a commitment to rebuilding trust and preserving the integrity of the relationship.

Continuous Nurturing

Trust is not static; it requires ongoing nurturing and maintenance to thrive. Partners should prioritize trust-building behaviors such as open communication, honesty, reliability, and empathy in daily interactions. By consistently demonstrating trustworthiness and acting with integrity, partners can deepen their bond, enhance emotional intimacy, and cultivate a relationship grounded in mutual trust and respect.

Conclusion

Trust is the bedrock of a healthy and fulfilling relationship, providing the stability, security, and emotional safety necessary for intimacy and connection to flourish. By prioritizing transparency, honesty, reliability, vulnerability, and forgiveness, partners can build and maintain trust, fostering a relationship characterized by mutual respect, understanding, and support.

Mutual Respect: Nurturing Equality and Understanding

Mutual respect forms the cornerstone of healthy and fulfilling relationships, fostering equality, empathy, and understanding between partners. In this chapter, we explore the importance of mutual respect in nurturing a strong and harmonious relationship, and strategies for cultivating respect and understanding within the partnership.

The Significance of Mutual Respect

Mutual respect is the recognition and appreciation of each other's worth, dignity, and autonomy. It involves treating each other with kindness, consideration, and empathy, and valuing each other's thoughts, feelings, and perspectives. Mutual respect creates a foundation of equality and understanding within the relationship, fostering trust, cooperation, and emotional intimacy.

Valuing Differences

In a respectful relationship, partners embrace and celebrate their differences rather than seeking to change or control each other. They recognize that each person brings unique strengths, experiences, and perspectives to the relationship, enriching the partnership with diversity and depth. By valuing and respecting each other's differences, partners create a dynamic and inclusive environment where individuality is celebrated and honored.

Open Communication and Active Listening

Open communication and active listening are essential for fostering mutual respect in a relationship. Partners should strive to communicate honestly and openly, expressing their thoughts, feelings, and needs with kindness and empathy. Equally important is the ability to listen attentively and empathetically, seeking to understand each other's perspective without judgment or defensiveness. By practicing open communication and active listening, partners demonstrate respect for each other's thoughts, feelings, and experiences, fostering a deeper sense of connection and understanding.

Setting Boundaries and Honoring Limits

Respecting each other's boundaries and honoring limits is crucial for maintaining a healthy balance in the relationship. Partners should communicate their needs, preferences, and boundaries clearly and assertively, and respect each other's autonomy and agency. Respecting boundaries demonstrates trust, empathy, and consideration, fostering a safe and supportive environment where partners feel respected and valued.

Empowering Each Other

In a respectful relationship, partners empower each other to pursue their goals, dreams, and aspirations, and support each other's personal growth and development. They celebrate each other's achievements, offer encouragement and validation, and provide a nurturing environment where each person can thrive and flourish. By empowering each other, partners demonstrate faith in each other's abilities and potential, and foster a sense of mutual respect and admiration.

Continuous Cultivation

Mutual respect is not static; it requires continuous cultivation and reinforcement to thrive. Partners should prioritize respect in their daily interactions, and actively seek to understand and appreciate each other's perspectives, experiences, and feelings. By consistently demonstrating kindness, empathy, and consideration, partners can nurture a relationship characterized by mutual respect, equality, and understanding.

Conclusion

Mutual respect is the foundation of a healthy and fulfilling relationship, fostering equality, empathy, and understanding between partners. By valuing differences, practicing open communication, setting boundaries, empowering each other, and cultivating respect in their daily interactions, partners can build a relationship grounded in mutual respect and admiration, and create a supportive and harmonious partnership that stands the test of time.

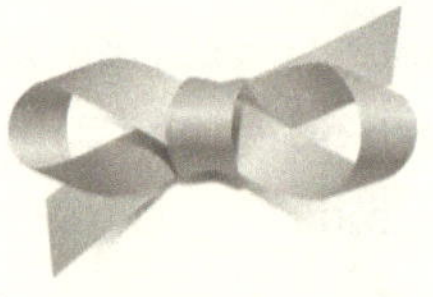

Chapter 3:

Understanding Yourself and Your Partner

Self-Awareness: Knowing Your Needs and Boundaries

Self-awareness is a fundamental aspect of personal growth and a key ingredient in cultivating healthy and fulfilling relationships. In this chapter, we explore the importance of self-awareness in understanding one's needs and boundaries, and how it contributes to the overall health and success of relationships.

Understanding Self-Awareness

Self-awareness is the ability to introspectively understand one's thoughts, feelings, values, and motivations. It involves being conscious of one's strengths, weaknesses, needs, and boundaries, and how they influence one's behavior and interactions with others. Self-awareness empowers individuals to make informed decisions, set meaningful goals, and navigate relationships with clarity and intentionality.

Identifying Your Needs

Understanding and articulating your needs is essential for fostering self-awareness and nurturing healthy relationships. Needs can encompass a wide range of physical, emotional, and psychological desires, such as the need for love, respect, validation, autonomy, and security. By identifying and communicating your needs to your partner, you can create a supportive environment where your needs are acknowledged, respected, and met, fostering a deeper sense of connection and fulfillment.

Establishing Personal Boundaries

Boundaries are the limits and guidelines that define the parameters of acceptable behavior in relationships. They serve to protect one's physical, emotional, and psychological well-being, and promote autonomy, self-respect, and healthy communication. Establishing clear and assertive boundaries communicates to your partner how you expect to be treated, what behavior is acceptable or unacceptable, and what your limits are. By honoring your boundaries and respecting those of your partner, you create a foundation of mutual respect and understanding within the relationship.

Exploring Triggers and Patterns

Self-awareness involves recognizing and understanding your triggers—events or situations that evoke strong emotional reactions—and patterns of behavior that may be detrimental to your well-being or relationships. By identifying your triggers and exploring the underlying beliefs, fears, and insecurities that contribute to them, you can develop healthier coping mechanisms and communication strategies. Similarly, recognizing recurring patterns of behavior or conflicts in your relationships can provide valuable insights into areas for personal growth and development.

Practicing Self-Reflection and Mindfulness

Self-awareness is cultivated through practices such as self-reflection and mindfulness, which involve observing your thoughts, emotions, and behaviors without judgment or attachment. Taking time for self-reflection allows you to gain clarity and insight into your inner world, deepen your understanding of yourself, and make conscious choices aligned with your values and goals. Mindfulness practices, such as meditation and mindfulness exercises, help you cultivate present-moment awareness and develop a greater sense of acceptance and compassion towards yourself and others.

Conclusion

Self-awareness is a foundational skill for fostering healthy and fulfilling relationships. By understanding your needs and boundaries, identifying triggers and patterns, and practicing self-reflection and mindfulness, you can cultivate a deeper understanding of yourself and your partner, and create a relationship characterized by mutual respect, empathy, and authenticity. Developing self-awareness empowers you to navigate relationships with clarity, intentionality, and emotional intelligence, fostering greater connection, intimacy, and fulfillment.

Understanding Your Partner: Empathy and Compassion

Empathy and compassion are essential qualities for fostering connection, intimacy, and mutual support in a relationship. In this chapter, we explore the importance of understanding your partner through empathy and compassion, and how these qualities contribute to the overall health and success of relationships.

The Role of Empathy and Compassion

Empathy is the ability to understand and share the feelings and perspectives of another person, while compassion is the desire to alleviate their suffering or distress. Together, these qualities form the foundation of understanding and connection in a relationship. By empathizing with your partner's experiences, thoughts, and emotions, and demonstrating compassion towards their struggles and challenges, you create a supportive and nurturing environment where trust, intimacy, and mutual respect can flourish.

Cultivating Empathy

Empathy is cultivated through active listening, perspective-taking, and genuine curiosity about your partner's experiences and emotions. It involves putting yourself in their shoes, seeking to understand their perspective without judgment or defensiveness, and validating their feelings and experiences. By practicing empathy, you demonstrate that you care about your partner's well-being and are invested in understanding their inner world, fostering a deeper sense of connection and emotional intimacy.

Expressing Compassion

BUILDING THE PERFECT RELATIONSHIP: A COMPREHENSIVE GUIDE

Compassion involves recognizing and responding to your partner's suffering or distress with kindness, empathy, and support. It entails offering comfort, validation, and reassurance during times of difficulty, and providing practical assistance or encouragement when needed. By expressing compassion towards your partner, you create a safe and nurturing space where they feel understood, valued, and supported, strengthening the bond between you.

Validating Feelings and Experiences

Validation is an important aspect of empathy and compassion, as it communicates to your partner that their feelings and experiences are valid, worthy of acknowledgment, and deserving of empathy and support. Validating your partner's feelings involves listening attentively, acknowledging their emotions without judgment or criticism, and expressing empathy and understanding. By validating your partner's feelings and experiences, you demonstrate that you respect and value their perspective, fostering trust, empathy, and emotional intimacy.

Navigating Differences with Empathy

Empathy and compassion are particularly important when navigating differences or conflicts in a relationship. By approaching disagreements with empathy and compassion, partners can foster understanding, empathy, and mutual respect, even in the midst of disagreement or discord. Empathizing with your partner's perspective, expressing compassion towards their feelings, and seeking common ground can help bridge differences and strengthen the connection between you.

Conclusion

Understanding your partner through empathy and compassion is essential for fostering connection, intimacy, and mutual support in a relationship. By cultivating empathy, expressing compassion, validating feelings and experiences, and navigating differences with empathy, partners can create a relationship characterized by understanding, empathy, and emotional intimacy. Developing these qualities empowers partners to support each other through life's challenges, celebrate each other's successes, and navigate the ups and downs of life with grace and compassion.

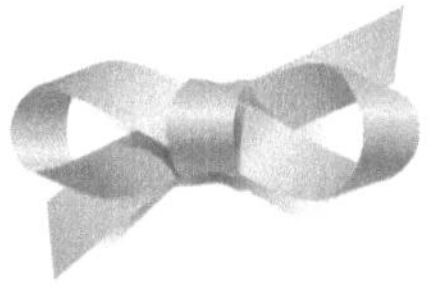

Chapter 4:

Cultivating Intimacy

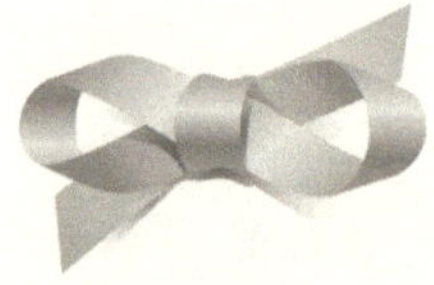

Emotional Intimacy: Sharing Vulnerability

Emotional intimacy is the deep connection that arises from sharing one's innermost thoughts, feelings, and experiences with a partner. In this chapter, we explore the importance of emotional intimacy in a relationship, and how sharing vulnerability can deepen the bond between partners.

Understanding Emotional Intimacy

Emotional intimacy is the foundation of a strong and fulfilling relationship, providing a sense of closeness, connection, and mutual understanding between partners. It involves sharing one's fears, hopes, dreams, and insecurities with a partner, and feeling safe being vulnerable and authentic in their presence. Emotional intimacy fosters trust, empathy, and mutual support, creating a deep and meaningful connection that transcends physical proximity.

Creating a Safe Space for Vulnerability

Creating a safe and supportive environment where partners feel comfortable being vulnerable is essential for nurturing emotional intimacy. Partners should cultivate an atmosphere of trust, acceptance, and non-judgment, where each person feels valued, respected, and understood. By actively listening, providing validation, and offering empathy and support, partners can create a safe space where vulnerability is welcomed and celebrated.

Sharing Deep Thoughts and Feelings

Sharing deep thoughts and feelings is central to building emotional intimacy in a relationship. Partners should be willing to open up about their innermost thoughts, fears, and desires, and to listen with empathy and understanding when their partner does the same. By sharing vulnerabilities, partners deepen their emotional connection, strengthen their bond, and cultivate a sense of intimacy and closeness that enhances the quality of their relationship.

Navigating Difficult Conversations

Difficult conversations are an inevitable part of any relationship, but they can also be opportunities for growth and deepening emotional intimacy. When navigating sensitive topics or conflicts, partners should approach conversations with empathy, openness, and a willingness to listen and understand each other's perspective. By communicating respectfully and compassionately, partners can address issues constructively, strengthen their bond, and build trust and intimacy in the process.

Building Trust Through Vulnerability

Sharing vulnerability is a powerful way to build trust in a relationship. When partners feel safe being vulnerable with each other, they demonstrate trust in their partner's ability to handle their emotions with care and compassion. By responding with empathy, validation, and support, partners reinforce trust and deepen their emotional connection, creating a strong foundation for intimacy and closeness.

Conclusion

Emotional intimacy is the heart of a fulfilling and meaningful relationship, providing partners with a deep sense of connection, understanding, and mutual support. By creating a safe space for vulnerability, sharing deep thoughts and feelings, navigating difficult conversations with empathy, and building trust through vulnerability, partners can cultivate a relationship characterized by intimacy, trust, and emotional depth. Sharing vulnerability fosters a deep and meaningful connection that enriches the relationship and enhances the overall quality of life for both partners.

Physical Intimacy: Nurturing Affection and Desire

Physical intimacy plays a vital role in relationships, fostering closeness, connection, and passion between partners. In this chapter, we explore the importance of physical intimacy, and how nurturing affection and desire can enhance the bond between partners.

Understanding Physical Intimacy

Physical intimacy encompasses a wide range of behaviors and expressions, including touch, affection, sexual activity, and non-verbal communication. It serves as a powerful means of expressing love, desire, and connection between partners, and plays a crucial role in building and maintaining a healthy and fulfilling relationship.

Expressing Affection

Expressing affection is an essential component of physical intimacy, demonstrating love, appreciation, and care for your partner through gestures, words, and touch. Simple acts of affection, such as holding hands, cuddling, kissing, and hugging, communicate warmth, closeness, and connection, fostering a sense of security and emotional intimacy between partners.

Fostering Desire

Desire is an integral part of physical intimacy, fueling passion, excitement, and sexual attraction between partners. Fostering desire involves cultivating a sense of anticipation, mystery, and adventure in the relationship, and prioritizing intimacy and connection in daily interactions. By expressing desire for your partner, initiating physical contact, and exploring each other's desires and fantasies, partners can reignite the spark and deepen their bond.

BUILDING THE PERFECT RELATIONSHIP: A COMPREHENSIVE GUIDE

Communication and Consent

Effective communication and mutual consent are essential for fostering a healthy and satisfying physical relationship. Partners should feel comfortable discussing their desires, boundaries, and preferences openly and honestly, and respecting each other's autonomy and agency. By communicating openly, listening attentively, and seeking consent enthusiastically, partners can create a safe and respectful environment where physical intimacy can flourish.

Exploring Sensuality and Connection

Physical intimacy goes beyond sexual activity; it encompasses the full spectrum of sensory experiences that foster connection and pleasure between partners. Exploring sensuality involves engaging all the senses—touch, taste, smell, sight, and sound—to heighten arousal, deepen connection, and enhance the overall experience of intimacy. By prioritizing sensual experiences, partners can nurture a deeper sense of connection and passion in their relationship.

Overcoming Challenges

Physical intimacy may face challenges over time, such as stress, fatigue, or changes in desire or libido. However, by prioritizing communication, empathy, and creativity, partners can overcome these challenges and maintain a satisfying and fulfilling physical relationship. Whether through exploring new activities, experimenting with different techniques, or seeking support from a therapist or counselor, partners can navigate obstacles and strengthen their bond.

Conclusion

Physical intimacy is a vital component of a healthy and fulfilling relationship, providing partners with a means of expressing love, desire, and connection. By nurturing affection, fostering desire, prioritizing communication, and consent, exploring sensuality and connection, and overcoming challenges together, partners can cultivate a deep and satisfying physical relationship that enhances their overall connection and quality of life. Physical intimacy serves as a powerful tool for strengthening the bond between partners, fostering closeness, passion, and mutual fulfillment.

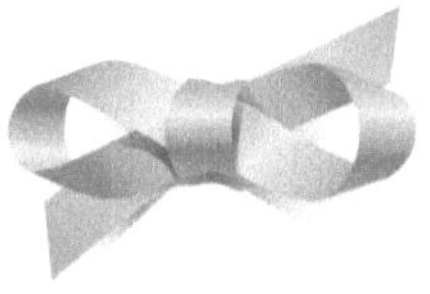

Chapter 5:

Navigating Challenges Together

Conflict Resolution: Turning Disagreements into Opportunities for Growth

Conflict is a natural and inevitable part of any relationship, but how it is managed can either strengthen or weaken the bond between partners. In this chapter, we explore the importance of effective conflict resolution in fostering growth and deepening the connection between partners.

Understanding Conflict

Conflict arises when there is a disagreement or clash of interests between partners. It can manifest in various forms, including differences in opinions, values, expectations, and behaviors. While conflict may be uncomfortable or challenging, it also presents an opportunity for growth, learning, and strengthening the relationship if approached constructively.

Changing Perspectives

Effective conflict resolution begins with a shift in perspective, viewing disagreements not as threats to the relationship, but as opportunities for growth and deeper understanding. By reframing conflict as a natural and normal aspect of any partnership, partners can approach disagreements with curiosity, openness, and a willingness to listen and learn from each other.

Active Listening and Empathetic Communication

Active listening and empathetic communication are crucial skills for resolving conflict constructively. Partners should strive to listen attentively to each other's perspectives, seeking to understand the underlying emotions, needs, and concerns driving the disagreement. By expressing empathy, validation, and understanding, partners create a safe and supportive environment where both parties feel heard and respected.

Seeking Common Ground

Finding common ground is essential for resolving conflict and moving forward together. Partners should identify shared values, goals, and interests that they can align on, and focus on areas of agreement rather than dwelling on differences. By emphasizing areas of commonality and working towards mutually beneficial solutions, partners can strengthen their bond and build trust and cooperation in the relationship.

Compromise and Collaboration

Compromise and collaboration are key components of effective conflict resolution. Partners should be willing to make concessions and find middle ground in order to reach a resolution that satisfies both parties. Collaboration involves working together as a team, brainstorming creative solutions, and exploring different perspectives in pursuit of a win-win outcome. By prioritizing the well-being of the relationship over individual needs or desires, partners can foster a spirit of cooperation and unity.

Learning and Growth

Conflict resolution offers valuable opportunities for learning and personal growth. Partners can gain insights into their own triggers, biases, and communication patterns, as well as those of their partner. By reflecting on past conflicts, identifying areas for improvement, and implementing strategies for more effective communication and conflict resolution, partners can strengthen their relationship and deepen their connection over time.

Conclusion

Conflict resolution is an essential skill for fostering growth, learning, and deeper connection in a relationship. By approaching disagreements with openness, empathy, and a willingness to collaborate, partners can transform conflict into an opportunity for growth and strengthen their bond in the process. Effective conflict resolution requires active listening, empathetic communication, seeking common ground, compromise, and a commitment to ongoing learning and growth. Through these efforts, partners can navigate conflicts constructively, strengthen their relationship, and emerge stronger and more resilient together.

Managing Stress and External Pressures

In the fast-paced world we live in, managing stress and external pressures is essential for maintaining a healthy and thriving relationship. In this chapter, we explore the impact of stress on relationships and provide strategies for effectively managing external pressures together.

Understanding the Impact of Stress

Stress is a natural response to challenging or demanding situations, but prolonged or excessive stress can take a toll on mental, emotional, and physical well-being, as well as on relationships. External pressures such as work, financial concerns, family obligations, and societal expectations can exacerbate stress levels and strain the relationship if left unchecked.

Open Communication

Open communication is crucial for managing stress and external pressures in a relationship. Partners should feel comfortable expressing their concerns, fears, and anxieties with each other, and offering support and validation in return. By sharing the burden of stress and problem-solving together, partners can strengthen their bond and navigate challenges more effectively.

Setting Boundaries

Setting boundaries is essential for protecting the relationship from the negative effects of external pressures. Partners should discuss and agree on boundaries around work, social commitments, family obligations, and other stressors to ensure that their relationship remains a priority. By respecting each other's boundaries and honoring their need for space and self-care, partners can create a supportive environment where they can recharge and rejuvenate.

Prioritizing Self-Care

Prioritizing self-care is essential for managing stress and maintaining emotional well-being. Partners should make time for activities that bring them joy, relaxation, and fulfillment, whether it's exercise, hobbies, spending time with loved ones, or engaging in mindfulness practices. By taking care of themselves, partners can better cope with stress and be more present and supportive in their relationship.

Seeking Support

Seeking support from friends, family, or a therapist can be beneficial for managing stress and external pressures in a relationship. Partners should feel comfortable reaching out for help when needed and offering support to each other in times of difficulty. By seeking professional help or joining support groups, partners can gain valuable insights, tools, and strategies for coping with stress and strengthening their relationship.

Creating Rituals of Connection

Creating rituals of connection can help partners stay connected and grounded amidst external pressures. Whether it's a weekly date night, a daily check-in, or a morning gratitude practice, these rituals provide opportunities for partners to reconnect, communicate, and support each other. By prioritizing quality time together, partners can nurture their bond and weather external pressures more effectively.

Conclusion

Managing stress and external pressures is essential for maintaining a healthy and thriving relationship. By fostering open communication, setting boundaries, prioritizing self-care, seeking support, and creating rituals of connection, partners can navigate challenges together and emerge stronger and more resilient. Through mutual support, understanding, and collaboration, partners can build a relationship that withstands the ups and downs of life and flourishes in the face of adversity.

Chapter 6:

Building a Shared Vision

Goal Setting: Aligning Ambitions and Dreams

Goal setting is a powerful tool for couples to align their ambitions, dreams, and aspirations, and work towards a shared vision for the future. In this chapter, we explore the importance of setting goals together and provide strategies for achieving mutual fulfillment and success.

Understanding Shared Goals

Shared goals are aspirations or objectives that partners work towards together, whether they relate to career, finances, family, personal growth, or lifestyle. Setting shared goals fosters alignment, cooperation, and mutual support in the relationship, as partners collaborate to achieve common objectives and aspirations.

Creating a Shared Vision

Creating a shared vision involves discussing and articulating your individual values, priorities, and aspirations, and identifying areas of alignment and overlap. Partners should take time to reflect on their dreams and goals and explore how they can support each other in achieving them. By creating a shared vision for the future, partners lay the foundation for collaboration, mutual support, and shared success.

Setting SMART Goals

Setting SMART goals—specific, measurable, achievable, relevant, and time-bound—is essential for turning aspirations into actionable plans. Partners should work together to define clear and concrete goals that are aligned with their shared vision and values. By breaking down larger goals into smaller, manageable steps, partners can track progress, stay motivated, and celebrate achievements together.

Communicating and Collaborating

Effective communication and collaboration are key for setting and achieving shared goals. Partners should openly discuss their aspirations, concerns, and expectations, and actively listen to each other's perspectives and needs. By communicating openly and collaboratively, partners can identify areas of overlap and synergy, and develop strategies for working together towards shared objectives.

Supporting Each Other's Growth

Supporting each other's growth and development is essential for achieving shared goals and fostering mutual fulfillment. Partners should encourage and empower each other to pursue their passions, interests, and ambitions, and provide emotional, practical, and moral support along the way. By celebrating each other's successes and offering encouragement during setbacks, partners create a supportive environment where both individuals can thrive and grow.

Evaluating and Adjusting

Regularly evaluating progress towards shared goals and adjusting plans as needed is crucial for staying on track and maintaining momentum. Partners should periodically review their goals, assess what's working and what's not, and adjust as necessary. By staying flexible and adaptable, partners can navigate challenges and setbacks with resilience and determination and continue moving forward towards their shared vision.

Conclusion

Goal setting is a powerful tool for aligning ambitions and dreams in a relationship, fostering cooperation, mutual support, and shared success. By creating a shared vision, setting SMART goals, communicating openly and collaboratively, supporting each other's growth, and regularly evaluating progress, partners can achieve mutual fulfillment and build a relationship that thrives on shared aspirations and achievements. Through shared goals, partners deepen their bond, strengthen their connection, and create a future filled with mutual success and happiness.

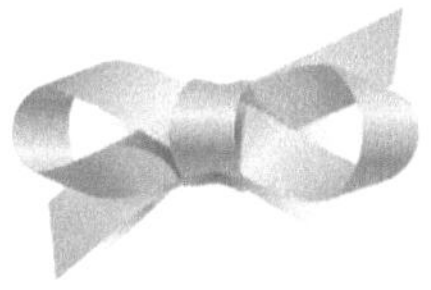

Compromise and Collaboration: Fostering Teamwork

Compromise and collaboration are essential skills for building a strong and resilient relationship. In this chapter, we explore the importance of compromise and collaboration in fostering teamwork and provide strategies for navigating differences and working together towards common goals.

Understanding Compromise

Compromise involves finding a middle ground or reaching an agreement that satisfies the needs and interests of both partners, even if it requires making concessions or sacrifices. Compromise is not about winning or losing, but about finding mutually acceptable solutions that honor the needs and perspectives of both individuals.

Embracing Collaboration

Collaboration is the process of working together towards a shared goal or objective, leveraging each other's strengths, skills, and resources to achieve mutual success. Collaboration involves communication, cooperation, and a willingness to listen to and respect each other's ideas and contributions.

Effective Communication

Effective communication is essential for successful compromise and collaboration. Partners should openly express their needs, concerns, and preferences, and actively listen to each other's perspectives without judgment or defensiveness. By fostering open and honest communication, partners can build trust, understanding, and mutual respect, laying the foundation for effective compromise and collaboration.

Identifying Common Goals

Identifying common goals is essential for fostering collaboration and teamwork in a relationship. Partners should discuss their individual aspirations, values, and priorities, and identify areas of overlap and alignment. By working towards shared goals, partners can strengthen their bond, deepen their connection, and achieve greater fulfillment and success together.

Seeking Win-Win Solutions

In compromise and collaboration, the goal should be to seek win-win solutions that satisfy the needs and interests of both partners. Partners should approach disagreements with a mindset of curiosity, creativity, and flexibility, exploring multiple options and brainstorming creative solutions. By prioritizing cooperation and mutual benefit, partners can find compromises that honor both individuals' perspectives and needs.

Respecting Each Other's Boundaries

Respecting each other's boundaries is essential for effective compromise and collaboration. Partners should acknowledge and honor each other's limits, preferences, and autonomy, and avoid pressuring or coercing each other into making concessions that feel uncomfortable or compromising. By respecting each other's boundaries, partners demonstrate trust, empathy, and consideration, fostering a supportive and respectful environment for compromise and collaboration.

Celebrating Successes Together

Celebrating successes together is an important aspect of fostering teamwork and collaboration in a relationship. Partners should acknowledge and celebrate each other's achievements, milestones, and contributions, and express gratitude and appreciation for their efforts. By celebrating successes together, partners reinforce their bond, boost morale, and cultivate a sense of shared accomplishment and pride in their partnership.

Conclusion

BUILDING THE PERFECT RELATIONSHIP: A COMPREHENSIVE GUIDE

Compromise and collaboration are essential skills for building a strong and resilient relationship. By embracing compromise, fostering collaboration, communicating effectively, identifying common goals, seeking win-win solutions, respecting each other's boundaries, and celebrating successes together, partners can cultivate a relationship characterized by teamwork, mutual support, and shared success. Through compromise and collaboration, partners deepen their bond, strengthen their connection, and build a relationship that thrives on cooperation, understanding, and mutual respect.

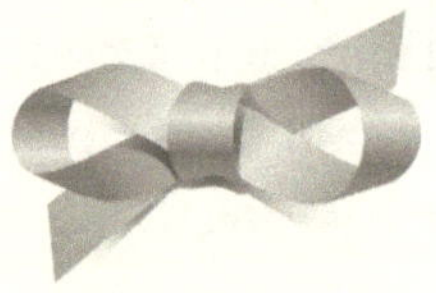

Chapter 7:

Sustaining the Relationship

Continual Growth and Development

In any successful and fulfilling relationship, continual growth and development are essential for maintaining vitality, deepening connection, and adapting to the ever-changing dynamics of life. In this chapter, we explore the importance of embracing growth and development individually and as a couple and provide strategies for nurturing personal and relational evolution.

Embracing Lifelong Learning

Lifelong learning is a cornerstone of personal and relational growth. Partners should approach life with a growth mindset, viewing challenges as opportunities for learning and self-improvement. By seeking out new experiences, acquiring new skills, and expanding their knowledge base, partners can continually evolve and enrich their lives individually and as a couple.

Supporting Personal Growth

Supporting each other's personal growth is essential for fostering a thriving relationship. Partners should encourage and empower each other to pursue their passions, interests, and goals, and provide emotional, practical, and moral support along the way. By celebrating each other's achievements, offering encouragement during setbacks, and providing constructive feedback, partners create a nurturing environment where both individuals can flourish and thrive.

Cultivating Relational Growth

Cultivating relational growth involves investing time and effort into nurturing the relationship and strengthening the bond between partners. This includes engaging in regular communication, expressing appreciation and gratitude, and making time for shared activities and experiences that deepen connection and intimacy. By prioritizing the relationship and actively working to enhance its quality, partners can create a partnership that continues to grow and evolve over time.

Embracing Change

Change is inevitable in any relationship, and embracing change is essential for growth and development. Partners should be open to new experiences, perspectives, and opportunities for growth, and be willing to adapt and evolve together as individuals and as a couple. By embracing change with curiosity, flexibility, and a spirit of adventure, partners can navigate life's transitions with grace and resilience, and emerge stronger and more connected in the process.

Setting and Pursuing Goals Together

Setting and pursuing goals together is a powerful way to foster growth and development in a relationship. Partners should discuss their aspirations, values, and priorities, and identify shared goals that they can work towards together. By collaborating on shared objectives, supporting each other's efforts, and celebrating achievements together, partners can strengthen their bond, deepen their connection, and achieve greater fulfillment and success as a couple.

Reflecting and Reassessing

Regularly reflecting on the relationship and reassessing individual and shared goals is essential for continual growth and development. Partners should take time to evaluate what's working well, what could be improved, and what goals they want to set for the future. By engaging in open and honest communication, partners can identify areas for growth, set intentions for personal and relational development, and take proactive steps towards achieving their goals together.

Conclusion

Continual growth and development are essential for maintaining a healthy, fulfilling, and thriving relationship. By embracing lifelong learning, supporting each other's personal growth, cultivating relational growth, embracing change, setting and pursuing goals together, and regularly reflecting and reassessing, partners can nurture a partnership that evolves and deepens over time. Through a commitment to growth and development, partners can create a relationship that is resilient, vibrant, and deeply fulfilling for both individuals involved.

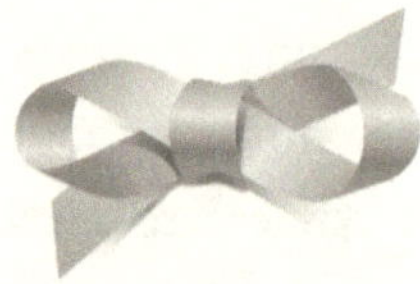

Maintaining Spark and Passion

In any long-term relationship, maintaining the spark and passion that initially brought partners together is crucial for sustaining intimacy, connection, and fulfillment. In this chapter, we explore strategies for reigniting the flame and keeping the passion alive in a relationship.

Prioritize Quality Time Together

Quality time together is essential for maintaining intimacy and connection in a relationship. Partners should make time for shared activities, dates, and experiences that bring joy, excitement, and closeness. Whether it's trying new things, exploring shared interests, or simply enjoying each other's company, prioritizing quality time together helps keep the spark alive and strengthens the bond between partners.

Keep Romance Alive

Romance plays a key role in keeping the passion alive in a relationship. Partners should make an effort to express affection, appreciation, and admiration for each other regularly. This can include gestures such as writing love notes, surprising each other with thoughtful gifts, or planning romantic getaways. By nurturing romance and creating opportunities for intimacy, partners can reignite the flame and deepen their connection.

Embrace Spontaneity and Adventure

Spontaneity and adventure inject excitement and novelty into a relationship, keeping things fresh and vibrant. Partners should be open to trying new things, stepping out of their comfort zones, and embracing unexpected opportunities for adventure together. Whether it's exploring new hobbies, taking spontaneous road trips, or trying new activities in the bedroom, embracing spontaneity and adventure helps keep the passion alive and strengthens the bond between partners.

Communicate Openly About Desires and Fantasies

Open communication about desires and fantasies is essential for maintaining passion and intimacy in a relationship. Partners should feel comfortable expressing their wants, needs, and fantasies with each other without fear of judgment or rejection. By communicating openly and non-judgmentally, partners can explore each other's desires and fantasies, and find new ways to keep the passion alive and reignite the flame.

Prioritize Physical Intimacy

Physical intimacy is a powerful way to maintain passion and connection in a relationship. Partners should prioritize intimacy and make time for physical affection, closeness, and sexual intimacy on a regular basis. This can include activities such as cuddling, kissing, and lovemaking, as well as exploring new ways to pleasure and connect with each other physically. By prioritizing physical intimacy, partners can keep the spark alive and deepen their bond.

Invest in Self-Care and Personal Growth

Investing in self-care and personal growth is essential for maintaining passion and vitality in a relationship. Partners should prioritize their own well-being and happiness, pursuing activities and interests that bring them joy, fulfillment, and a sense of purpose. By taking care of themselves and investing in their own growth and development, partners can bring more energy, enthusiasm, and passion to the relationship, enriching the connection with their partner in the process.

Conclusion

Maintaining the spark and passion in a relationship requires effort, intentionality, and creativity. By prioritizing quality time together, keeping romance alive, embracing spontaneity and adventure, communicating openly about desires and fantasies, prioritizing physical intimacy, and investing in self-care and personal growth, partners can keep the flame burning bright and deepen their connection over time.

Through a commitment to nurturing passion and intimacy, partners can create a relationship that is vibrant, fulfilling, and deeply satisfying for both individuals involved.

Chapter 8:

Overcoming Common Relationship Pitfalls

Communication Breakdowns

Effective communication is the cornerstone of a healthy and thriving relationship. However, communication breakdowns can occur, leading to misunderstandings, conflict, and emotional distance between partners. In this chapter, we explore the common causes of communication breakdowns and provide strategies for overcoming them.

Causes of Communication Breakdowns

1. **Poor Listening:** When partners are not actively listening to each other, misunderstandings and misinterpretations can arise, leading to communication breakdowns.

2. **Assumptions and Misinterpretations:** Making assumptions or interpreting your partner's words or actions incorrectly can lead to misunderstandings and communication breakdowns.

3. **Emotional Reactivity:** Reacting emotionally to your partner's words or actions without pausing to consider their perspective can escalate conflict and lead to communication breakdowns.

4. **Lack of Clarity:** Vague or unclear communication can lead to confusion and misunderstanding between partners, resulting in communication breakdowns.

5. **Avoidance of Difficult Conversations:** Avoiding difficult conversations or sweeping issues under the rug can lead to unresolved conflicts and communication breakdowns.

6. **Communication Styles:** Differences in communication styles, such as one partner being more passive while the other is more assertive, can lead to communication breakdowns if not

addressed.

7. **Strategies for Overcoming Communication Breakdowns**

8. **Practice Active Listening:** Make a conscious effort to actively listen to your partner without interrupting or jumping to conclusions. Paraphrase what your partner has said to ensure understanding before responding.

9. **Clarify Intentions and Assumptions:** Clarify any assumptions or misunderstandings by asking questions and seeking clarification from your partner. Avoid making assumptions about their intentions or motivations.

10. **Manage Emotions:** Take a break and manage your emotions if you find yourself becoming reactive during a conversation. Practice deep breathing or mindfulness techniques to calm yourself before continuing the discussion.

11. **Be Clear and Direct:** Communicate your thoughts, feelings, and needs clearly and directly to your partner. Use "I" statements to express yourself without blaming or accusing your partner.

12. **Address Issues Promptly:** Address issues and concerns promptly rather than letting them fester and grow into larger problems. Schedule regular check-ins to discuss any issues or concerns that arise in the relationship.

13. **Understand Different Communication Styles:** Take the time to understand and appreciate your partner's communication style and communicate in a way that resonates with them. Practice empathy and adaptability in your communication approach.

14. **Seek Professional Help:** If communication breakdowns persist despite your best efforts, consider seeking the help of a couple's therapist or counselor. A trained professional can provide guidance and support in improving communication and resolving conflicts in the relationship.

Conclusion

Communication breakdowns are common in relationships but can be overcome with awareness, effort, and effective communication strategies. By practicing active listening, clarifying assumptions, managing emotions, being clear and direct, addressing issues promptly, understanding different communication styles, and seeking professional help when needed, partners can navigate communication breakdowns and strengthen their connection with each other. Through open and honest communication, partners can build trust, resolve conflicts, and foster a deeper understanding and appreciation for each other, ultimately leading to a stronger and more fulfilling relationship.

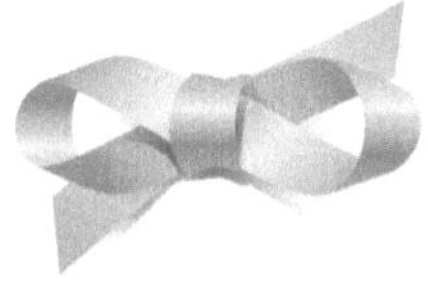

Trust Issues

Trust is the foundation of any healthy and thriving relationship. However, trust issues can arise due to past experiences, insecurities, or breaches of trust within the relationship itself. In this chapter, we explore the common causes of trust issues and provide strategies for rebuilding trust and strengthening the bond between partners.

Causes of Trust Issues

1. **Past Trauma or Betrayal:** Previous experiences of betrayal or trauma, whether in past relationships or childhood, can lead to trust issues in current relationships.
2. **Insecurities:** Personal insecurities or low self-esteem can contribute to trust issues, as individuals may struggle to trust their partner's intentions or fidelity.
3. **Lack of Communication:** Poor communication or a lack of transparency in the relationship can erode trust over time, as partners may feel uncertain or suspicious about each other's actions or motives.
4. **Jealousy and Possessiveness:** Excessive jealousy or possessiveness can breed mistrust in a relationship, as partners may feel threatened or insecure about their partner's interactions with others.
5. **Broken Promises or Lies:** Instances of broken promises or lies, whether big or small, can undermine trust and credibility in the relationship, leading to feelings of betrayal and resentment.
6. **Emotional Infidelity:** Emotional infidelity, such as forming close emotional bonds with someone outside the relationship,

can damage trust as much as physical infidelity, as partners may feel neglected or replaced.

7. **Strategies for Rebuilding Trust**

8. **Open and Honest Communication:** Foster open and honest communication in the relationship, allowing both partners to express their feelings, concerns, and needs without fear of judgment or reprisal.

9. **Transparency and Consistency:** Be transparent and consistent in your actions and words, demonstrating reliability, integrity, and accountability in the relationship.

10. **Setting Boundaries:** Establish clear boundaries and expectations in the relationship, respecting each other's autonomy and privacy while maintaining a commitment to honesty and fidelity.

11. **Addressing Past Hurts:** Acknowledge and address any past hurts or betrayals that may have contributed to trust issues in the relationship, seeking closure and forgiveness where possible.

12. **Building Emotional Connection:** Invest time and effort into building emotional connection and intimacy with your partner, strengthening the bond of trust and mutual support between you.

13. **Seeking Professional Help:** If trust issues persist despite your best efforts, consider seeking the guidance of a couple's therapist or counselor. A trained professional can provide support and guidance in navigating trust issues and rebuilding trust in the relationship.

Conclusion

Trust issues can be challenging to navigate, but with patience, understanding, and effort, they can be overcome. By fostering open and honest communication, practicing transparency and consistency, setting healthy boundaries, addressing past hurts, building emotional connection, and seeking professional help when needed, partners can rebuild trust and strengthen their bond. Through a commitment to honesty, integrity, and mutual respect, partners can create a relationship grounded in trust, understanding, and resilience, ultimately leading to greater intimacy, connection, and fulfillment for both individuals involved.

Intimacy Challenges

Intimacy is a cornerstone of a healthy and fulfilling relationship, encompassing emotional, physical, and sexual connection between partners. However, various challenges can arise that impact intimacy in a relationship. In this chapter, we explore common intimacy challenges and provide strategies for overcoming them to cultivate a deeper and more meaningful connection with your partner.

Common Intimacy Challenges

1. **Communication Issues:** Poor communication can hinder emotional intimacy, leading to misunderstandings, unresolved conflicts, and feelings of distance between partners.
2. **Physical Disconnection:** Physical intimacy challenges, such as lack of affection, sexual dissatisfaction, or differences in libido, can strain the emotional bond between partners.
3. **Emotional Distance:** Emotional intimacy challenges, such as feeling emotionally disconnected or emotionally unavailable, can create barriers to closeness and vulnerability in the relationship.
4. **Stress and External Pressures:** External stressors, such as work, finances, or family obligations, can impact intimacy by increasing tension, reducing quality time together, and causing partners to prioritize other concerns over their relationship.
5. **Trust Issues:** Trust issues, such as jealousy, insecurity, or past betrayals, can erode intimacy by creating feelings of fear, suspicion, or emotional guardedness between partners.
6. **Body Image and Self-Esteem:** Body image and self-esteem

issues can affect physical intimacy by causing individuals to feel self-conscious or insecure about their bodies, leading to avoidance of intimacy or discomfort during intimate moments.

Strategies for Overcoming Intimacy Challenges

1. **Prioritize Communication:** Foster open and honest communication with your partner, discussing your feelings, needs, and concerns related to intimacy in a safe and supportive environment.
2. **Create Quality Time Together:** Make time for shared activities, experiences, and conversations that promote emotional connection and intimacy between partners.
3. **Practice Emotional Vulnerability:** Cultivate emotional vulnerability by expressing your thoughts, feelings, and fears with your partner, and actively listening to and validating their experiences in return.
4. **Manage Stress Together:** Work together to manage stress and external pressures by setting boundaries, prioritizing self-care, and finding healthy ways to cope with stress as a team.
5. **Rebuild Trust:** Address trust issues openly and honestly, seeking to rebuild trust through transparency, consistency, and accountability in your actions and words.
6. **Boost Body Image and Self-Esteem:** Support each other in boosting body image and self-esteem by offering compliments, encouragement, and reassurance, and refraining from criticizing or judging each other's appearance.

Conclusion

Intimacy challenges are a natural part of any relationship, but with effort, understanding, and commitment, they can be overcome. By prioritizing communication, creating quality time together, practicing emotional vulnerability, managing stress together, rebuilding trust, and boosting body image and self-esteem, partners can navigate intimacy challenges and cultivate a deeper and more fulfilling connection with each other. Through a shared commitment to intimacy and mutual support, partners can strengthen their bond, enhance their relationship satisfaction, and experience greater levels of intimacy and connection in their relationship

External Influences

External influences encompass a wide range of factors outside the relationship that can impact its dynamics, stability, and overall well-being. In this chapter, we explore various external influences and provide strategies for navigating them effectively to strengthen the bond between partners.

Types of External Influences

1. **Family Dynamics:** Family dynamics, including relationships with parents, siblings, and extended family members, can influence the dynamics of a romantic relationship and impact communication, decision-making, and conflict resolution within the partnership.

2. **Social Circle:** The social circle, including friends, acquaintances, and social networks, can exert influence on the relationship through shared activities, values, and expectations, as well as through opinions and advice offered by others.

3. **Work and Career:** Work and career-related factors, such as job stress, work-life balance, and career ambitions, can impact the relationship by affecting individual well-being, availability, and priorities within the partnership.

4. **Cultural and Societal Norms:** Cultural and societal norms, including gender roles, expectations around marriage and family, and attitudes towards relationships and intimacy, can shape the values, beliefs, and behaviors of partners within the relationship.

5. **Technology and Media:** Technology and media, including

social media, entertainment, and digital communication, can influence the relationship by shaping perceptions of reality, creating distractions, and impacting communication patterns and dynamics between partners.

Navigating External Influences

1. **Open Communication:** Foster open and honest communication with your partner about external influences, discussing how they impact the relationship and identifying strategies for managing them effectively together.
2. **Establish Boundaries:** Set boundaries around external influences, such as limiting time spent with certain family members or friends, establishing technology-free zones or times, and prioritizing quality time together as a couple.
3. **Prioritize Shared Values:** Prioritize shared values and goals within the relationship, aligning decisions and behaviors with mutual aspirations and beliefs rather than succumbing to external pressures or expectations.
4. **Support Each Other's Individual Growth:** Support each other's individual growth and development, including career aspirations, personal interests, and cultural or societal identities, while maintaining a strong connection and mutual support within the relationship.
5. **Seek Professional Guidance:** If external influences pose significant challenges or conflicts within the relationship, consider seeking the guidance of a couple's therapist or counselor. A trained professional can provide support, perspective, and strategies for navigating external influences effectively and strengthening relationships.

Conclusion

BUILDING THE PERFECT RELATIONSHIP: A COMPREHENSIVE GUIDE

External influences are a natural part of any relationship, but with awareness, communication, and mutual support, partners can navigate them effectively and strengthen their bond. By fostering open communication, establishing boundaries, prioritizing shared values, supporting each other's individual growth, and seeking professional guidance when needed, partners can overcome external challenges and cultivate a relationship that thrives amidst external pressures. Through a shared commitment to navigating external influences together, partners can build resilience, deepen their connection, and create a relationship that is strong, resilient, and fulfilling for both individuals involved.

Chapter 9:

Tools and Techniques for Building the Perfect Relationship

Active Listening: The Key to Connection

Active listening is a fundamental skill in building strong and meaningful relationships. It involves fully engaging with what the other person is saying, understanding their perspective, and responding in a way that demonstrates empathy and respect. In this chapter, we explore the importance of active listening in relationships and provide strategies for enhancing this essential communication skill.

The Importance of Active Listening

1. **Enhanced Understanding:** Active listening allows you to gain a deeper understanding of your partner's thoughts, feelings, and perspectives. By actively engaging with what they are saying, you can grasp the underlying meaning behind their words and respond more effectively.

2. **Improved Communication:** Active listening fosters clearer and more effective communication between partners. When both individuals feel heard and understood, they are more likely to communicate openly and honestly, leading to greater trust and intimacy in the relationship.

3. **Validation and Empathy:** Active listening demonstrates validation and empathy towards your partner's experiences and emotions. By showing that you are attentive and empathetic to their needs, you strengthen the emotional connection and create a supportive environment for sharing and vulnerability.

4. **Conflict Resolution:** Active listening plays a crucial role in resolving conflicts and disagreements within the relationship. By listening attentively to your partner's perspective without

judgment or defensiveness, you can de-escalate tension and work towards finding mutually acceptable solutions.

Strategies for Practicing Active Listening

1. **Give Your Full Attention:** When your partner is speaking, give them your full attention. Put away distractions such as phones or electronic devices, make eye contact, and focus on what they are saying without interrupting.

2. **Show Empathy and Understanding:** Demonstrate empathy and understanding towards your partner's emotions and experiences. Validate their feelings by acknowledging their perspective and expressing empathy for what they are going through.

3. **Use Reflective Listening:** Practice reflective listening by paraphrasing and summarizing what your partner has said to ensure understanding. Repeat back key points and ask clarifying questions to demonstrate that you are actively engaged in the conversation.

4. **Avoid Judgment and Defensiveness:** Avoid jumping to conclusions or making judgments about your partner's thoughts or feelings. Create a non-judgmental space where they feel safe to express themselves openly without fear of criticism or rejection.

5. **Validate Feelings:** Validate your partner's feelings by acknowledging their emotions and expressing empathy for their experiences. Even if you don't agree with their perspective, validate their right to feel the way they do and offer support and understanding.

6. **Practice Patience and Presence:** Be patient and present during conversations with your partner. Avoid rushing to respond or jumping to conclusions, and instead, take the time to fully absorb what they are saying before offering your own

perspective.

Conclusion

Active listening is a powerful tool for building trust, understanding, and connection in relationships. By practicing active listening, you can enhance communication, foster empathy and validation, and create a supportive environment where both partners feel heard and understood. Through patience, presence, and empathy, active listening strengthens the emotional bond between partners and lays the foundation for a more fulfilling and harmonious relationship.

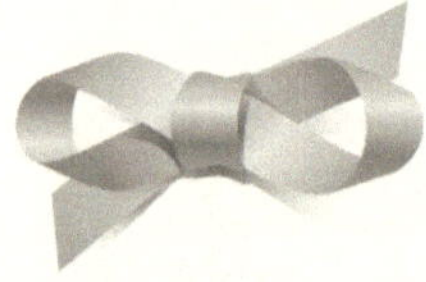

Effective Communication Strategies

Effective communication is the cornerstone of a healthy and thriving relationship. It involves more than just speaking; it encompasses active listening, empathy, and clarity in conveying thoughts and feelings. In this chapter, we explore various effective communication strategies that can strengthen connections, resolve conflicts, and foster intimacy in relationships.

1. Active Listening

Active listening is a vital component of effective communication. It involves giving your full attention to your partner, understanding their perspective, and responding in a way that demonstrates empathy and validation. Practice active listening by making eye contact, paraphrasing what your partner says to ensure understanding, and asking clarifying questions to show interest and engagement.

2. Use "I" Statements

When expressing your thoughts or feelings, use "I" statements to take ownership of your emotions and experiences. For example, instead of saying, "You never listen to me," say, "I feel unheard when I don't feel listened to." "I" statements promote accountability and prevent blame or defensiveness, creating a safe space for open and honest communication.

3. Practice Empathy

Empathy is the ability to understand and share the feelings of another person. Show empathy towards your partner by validating their emotions, acknowledging their experiences, and expressing understanding and support. Reflect back what your partner is feeling and validate their perspective to strengthen the emotional connection and foster trust in the relationship.

4. Be Clear and Concise

When communicating with your partner, strive to be clear and concise in conveying your thoughts and feelings. Avoid vague or ambiguous language and instead, express yourself in a straightforward and direct manner. Clearly communicate your needs, preferences, and boundaries to ensure mutual understanding and prevent misunderstandings.

5. Practice Non-Verbal Communication

Non-verbal communication, such as body language, facial expressions, and tone of voice, plays a significant role in effective communication. Pay attention to your non-verbal cues and those of your partner to better understand their emotions and intentions. Maintain open body language, make eye contact, and use a calm and respectful tone of voice to convey empathy and sincerity.

6. Validate and Affirm

Validation and affirmation are essential components of effective communication. Validate your partner's feelings by acknowledging their emotions and expressing empathy for their experiences. Affirm their strengths, accomplishments, and contributions to the relationship to build confidence and strengthen the emotional bond between you.

7. Practice Problem-Solving Together

When faced with conflicts or challenges in the relationship, practice problem-solving together as a team. Approach issues with a collaborative mindset, listen to each other's perspectives, and work together to find mutually acceptable solutions. Focus on understanding the underlying needs and interests driving the conflict and seek compromises that honor both partners' values and preferences.

Conclusion

Effective communication is vital for building trust, understanding, and intimacy in relationships. By practicing active listening, using "I" statements, practicing empathy, being clear and concise, paying attention to non-verbal cues, validating, and affirming each other, and practicing problem-solving together, partners can enhance communication and strengthen their connection with each other. Through open and honest communication, couples can navigate challenges, resolve conflicts, and build a relationship grounded in mutual respect, trust, and love.

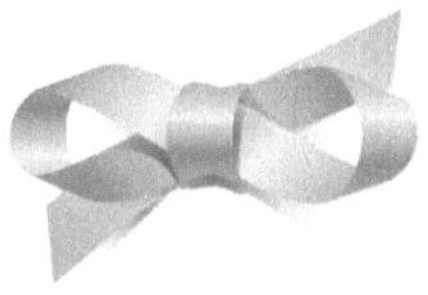

Conflict Resolution Models

Conflict is a natural and inevitable part of any relationship. How couples navigate and resolve conflicts can greatly impact the health and longevity of their partnership. In this chapter, we explore various conflict resolution models that couples can employ to address disagreements constructively and strengthen their bond.

1. The Win-Win Approach

The Win-Win approach, also known as collaborative or integrative negotiation, aims to find mutually beneficial solutions to conflicts. This model emphasizes open communication, active listening, and problem-solving to address the underlying needs and interests of both partners. By seeking win-win solutions, couples can preserve their relationship while also meeting each other's needs and desires.

2. The Lose-Lose Approach

The Lose-Lose approach, also known as avoidance or accommodation, involves minimizing conflict by sacrificing one's own needs or desires to maintain harmony in the relationship. While this approach may temporarily resolve conflicts, it can lead to feelings of resentment or dissatisfaction over time if one partner consistently suppresses their own needs. It's essential for couples to find a balance between accommodating each other and asserting their own needs to prevent long-term harm to the relationship.

3. The Win-Lose Approach

The Win-Lose approach, also known as competitive or distributive negotiation, involves one partner "winning" the conflict while the other "loses." This model can be detrimental to relationships as it prioritizes individual needs over the collective well-being of the partnership. While there may be situations where a Win-Lose approach is necessary, such as in emergencies or when safety is at risk, it's essential for couples to strive for mutual understanding and compromise whenever possible.

4. The Compromise Approach

The Compromise approach involves both partners making concessions to reach a middle ground and resolve conflicts. While compromise can be an effective way to address conflicts, it's essential for couples to avoid settling for "halfway" solutions that fail to fully address their underlying needs and interests. Instead, couples should strive to find creative solutions that honor both partners' priorities and values.

5. The Collaborative Approach

The Collaborative approach, also known as mediation or joint problem-solving, involves working together as a team to identify and address the root causes of conflicts. This model emphasizes active listening, empathy, and creativity to find mutually satisfying solutions that strengthen the relationship. By collaborating on conflict resolution, couples can deepen their understanding of each other and build a stronger foundation for future communication and problem-solving.

Choosing the Right Model

The most effective conflict resolution model for a particular situation will depend on the nature of the conflict, the personalities of the individuals involved, and the dynamics of the relationship. Couples may find that different approaches are more appropriate for different conflicts and may need to experiment with various models to find what works best for them. Regardless of the model chosen, the key is for couples to approach conflicts with respect, empathy, and a willingness to find solutions that honor both partners' needs and values.

Conclusion

Conflict resolution is an essential skill for maintaining a healthy and harmonious relationship. By familiarizing themselves with various conflict resolution models and practicing open communication, active listening, and empathy, couples can address conflicts constructively and strengthen their bond. Through collaboration, compromise, and a commitment to mutual understanding, couples can navigate conflicts with resilience and build a relationship grounded in trust, respect, and love.

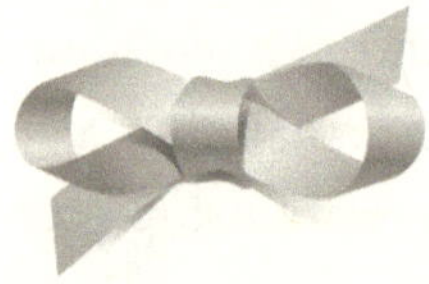

Relationship Building Exercises

Building a strong and resilient relationship requires intentional effort and investment from both partners. Relationship building exercises provide opportunities for couples to deepen their connection, enhance communication, and foster intimacy. In this chapter, we explore a variety of relationship building exercises that couples can engage in to strengthen their bond.

1. Relationship Vision Board

Create a relationship vision board together, outlining your shared goals, dreams, and aspirations for the future. Use images, words, and symbols to represent your vision for your relationship, and display it in a prominent place where you can revisit it regularly. This exercise helps couples align their aspirations and work towards a common vision for their partnership.

2. Appreciation Ritual

Set aside time each day to express appreciation for each other. Share one thing you appreciate about your partner, whether it's a specific action, trait, or quality. This simple ritual helps couples cultivate gratitude and reinforce positive aspects of their relationship, fostering a culture of appreciation and kindness.

3. Relationship Check-Ins

Schedule regular relationship check-ins to discuss your relationship's strengths, challenges, and goals. Use this time to reflect on what's working well, identify areas for improvement, and set intentions for growth together. Regular check-ins promote open communication and ensure that both partners feel heard and valued in the relationship.

4. Shared Journaling

BUILDING THE PERFECT RELATIONSHIP: A COMPREHENSIVE GUIDE

Start a shared journal where you and your partner can write about your thoughts, feelings, and experiences together. Use prompts or questions to spark conversation and reflection and take turns writing entries or responding to each other's entries. Shared journaling fosters intimacy and connection by providing a space for vulnerability and self-expression.

5. Love Languages Exercise

Take the love languages quiz together to identify your primary love languages and discuss how you prefer to give and receive love. Use this knowledge to tailor your expressions of love and affection to each other's preferences, strengthening your emotional connection and deepening your understanding of each other.

6. Relationship Rituals

Create relationship rituals that hold special meaning for you as a couple. Whether it's a weekly date night, a monthly adventure, or an annual tradition, establish rituals that you can look forward to and cherish together. These rituals strengthen your bond and create lasting memories that sustain your relationship through both good times and challenges.

7. Conflict Resolution Role-Play

Practice conflict resolution skills through role-playing scenarios that mimic real-life conflicts you may encounter. Take turns playing the role of both the initiator and the responder, and focus on using active listening, empathy, and problem-solving techniques to reach a resolution. Role-playing builds confidence and competence in addressing conflicts constructively.

8. Relationship Retreats

Plan occasional relationship retreats where you and your partner can disconnect from the distractions of daily life and focus on reconnecting with each other. Use this time to engage in meaningful conversations, participate in activities that bring you joy, and strengthen your bond through shared experiences.

Conclusion

Relationship building exercises provide valuable opportunities for couples to nurture their connection, enhance communication, and foster intimacy. By engaging in activities that promote mutual understanding, appreciation, and growth, couples can build a strong foundation for their relationship and navigate challenges with resilience and unity. Through intentional effort and investment in their partnership, couples can create a relationship that is fulfilling, supportive, and deeply meaningful for both individuals involved.

Chapter 10:

Conclusion

Recap of Key Points

Throughout this guide, we've explored various aspects of building and maintaining a healthy, fulfilling relationship. Here's a recap of the key points discussed:

1. **Importance of Relationship:** Relationships provide companionship, support, and growth opportunities, enriching our lives in profound ways.

2. **Understanding Dynamics of Healthy Relationships:** Healthy relationships are built on trust, communication, mutual respect, and shared values.

3. **Communication: The Key to Connection:** Effective communication involves active listening, empathy, clarity, and openness to understanding each other's perspectives.

4. **Trust: Building the Bedrock:** Trust is essential for the foundation of a strong relationship, developed through honesty, reliability, and consistency.

5. **Mutual Respect: Nurturing Equality and Understanding:** Respect your partner's autonomy, opinions, and boundaries, fostering equality and understanding in the relationship.

6. **Self-awareness: Knowing Your Needs and Boundaries:** Understanding your own needs, boundaries, and values is crucial for fostering a healthy relationship with yourself and your partner.

7. **Understanding Your Partner: Empathy and Compassion:** Practice empathy and compassion towards your partner, seeking to understand their experiences, emotions, and perspectives.

8. **Emotional Intimacy: Sharing Vulnerability:** Emotional intimacy is cultivated through open communication, vulnerability, and mutual support, deepening the emotional bond between partners.

9. **Physical Intimacy: Nurturing Affection and Desire:** Physical intimacy involves affection, closeness, and sexual connection, enhancing the emotional and physical connection between partners.

10. **Conflict Resolution: Turning Disagreements into Opportunities for Growth:** Conflict is inevitable in relationships, but it can be resolved constructively through active listening, empathy, and collaborative problem-solving.

11. **Managing Stress and External Pressures:** Work together to manage stress and external pressures, prioritizing self-care, communication, and support in navigating challenges together.

12. **Goal Setting: Aligning Ambitions and Dreams:** Set shared goals and aspirations, supporting each other's growth and development while working towards common objectives.

13. **Compromise and Collaboration: Fostering Teamwork:** Practice compromise and collaboration in decision-making, respecting each other's needs and finding solutions that honor both partners.

14. **Continual Growth and Development:** Commit to personal and relational growth, embracing challenges, and learning from experiences to strengthen the relationship over time.

15. **Maintaining Spark and Passion:** Nurture romance, spontaneity, and shared experiences to keep the passion alive and deepen the connection with your partner.

16. **Communication Breakdowns:** Address communication breakdowns through active listening, clarification, and empathy, fostering understanding and resolution.

17. **Trust Issues:** Rebuild trust through transparency, consistency,

and accountability, addressing past hurts and fostering a culture of honesty and reliability.

18. **Intimacy Challenges:** Overcome intimacy challenges through open communication, empathy, and vulnerability, fostering deeper emotional and physical connection.

19. **External Influences:** Navigate external influences with open communication, boundary-setting, and mutual support, prioritizing the relationship amidst external pressures.

20. **Active Listening:** Practice active listening by giving full attention, showing empathy, and responding with understanding and validation to deepen connection and trust.

21. **Effective Communication Strategies:** Employ effective communication strategies such as "I" statements, empathy, clarity, and non-verbal communication to enhance understanding and connection.

22. **Conflict Resolution Models:** Utilize conflict resolution models such as win-win, compromise, and collaboration to address conflicts constructively and strengthen the relationship.

23. **Relationship Building Exercises:** Engage in relationship building exercises such as appreciation rituals, shared journaling, and conflict resolution role-play to deepen connection and foster intimacy.

Incorporating these key points into your relationship can help you and your partner build a strong, resilient, and fulfilling partnership grounded in mutual respect, trust, and love. Through intentional effort, communication, and mutual support, you can create a relationship that brings joy, growth, and fulfillment to both individuals involved.

Encouragement for Continued Growth and Development

In every relationship, the journey of growth and development is ongoing. Just as individuals evolve and change over time, so too do relationships. Here are some words of encouragement to inspire you and your partner to continue growing and evolving together:

1. **Embrace Change:** Change is a natural part of life and relationships. Embrace the opportunities for growth and learning that come with change, and approach them with curiosity and openness.

2. **Celebrate Progress:** Take time to celebrate the progress you've made together. Reflect on the challenges you've overcome, the milestones you've reached, and the lessons you've learned along the way.

3. **Set New Goals:** Keep setting new goals and aspirations for yourselves as individuals and as a couple. Whether it's personal development goals, relationship goals, or shared dreams for the future, having something to strive towards can keep your relationship vibrant and dynamic.

4. **Support Each Other:** Be each other's biggest cheerleaders and supporters. Encourage and uplift one another as you pursue your individual passions and ambitions and celebrate each other's successes along the way.

5. **Embrace Vulnerability:** Cultivate a culture of vulnerability and authenticity in your relationship. Share your fears, hopes, and dreams with each other, and create a safe space where you

can be your true selves without judgment or criticism.

6. **Keep Communicating:** Communication is key to continued growth and development in your relationship. Keep talking openly and honestly with each other, sharing your thoughts, feelings, and needs as they evolve over time.

7. **Seek New Experiences:** Step out of your comfort zones and seek new experiences together. Whether it's traveling to new places, trying new activities, or learning new skills, exploring the world together can deepen your connection and broaden your horizons.

8. **Practice Gratitude:** Cultivate a mindset of gratitude for the journey you've shared and the growth you've experienced together. Take time to express appreciation for each other and the blessings in your lives, fostering a sense of abundance and contentment.

9. **Learn from Challenges:** View challenges and setbacks as opportunities for growth and resilience. Approach them with a mindset of learning and adaptation, and trust in your ability to overcome obstacles together.

10. **Stay Committed:** Above all, stay committed to each other and to the journey of growth and development you're on together. Remember that relationships require effort, patience, and dedication, but the rewards of continued growth and deepening connection are immeasurable.

As you continue on your journey of growth and development together, remember that every step you take, every challenge you overcome, and every moment you share strengthens the bond between you. Keep supporting each other, keep communicating openly, and keep embracing the opportunities for growth and learning that come your way. With love, dedication, and a commitment to each other's growth and happiness, your relationship will continue to flourish and thrive for years to come.

Don't miss out!

Visit the website below and you can sign up to receive emails whenever Jackquelin Grant publishes a new book. There's no charge and no obligation.

https://books2read.com/r/B-A-KSAEB-DRMXC

BOOKS 2 READ

Connecting independent readers to independent writers.